Visitors come from far and wide to see Guardian at Six Bells. All of us at Blaenau Gwent County Borough Council are justifiably proud of this iconic work of public art.

It is not only a fitting memorial to the 45 miners who lost their lives on that tragic day in 1960, but a tribute to those loved ones who were left behind.

Now set in a tranquil garden it gives visitors the opportunity to contemplate the past while admiring the lovely scenery. It is amazing how nature has reclaimed the beauty that preceded the industrial age.

Hedley McCarthy, B.A. (Hons)
Leader of Blaenau Gwent County Borough Council

Following an approach from The Abertillery and Llanhilleth District Community Council, Six Bells Communities First explored the potential to create a new miner's memorial with the local community. It quickly became apparent that the 1960 disaster was still very much a part of people's lives.

The project aimed to enable people affected by the disaster on the 28th June 1960 to create a personal and fitting tribute to those 45 men who lost their lives.

Initially a small project, it grew into one which involved over 400 family members, Mines Rescue, former miners, people who were school children and watched their friends being called out of class, surface workers, St. John's Ambulance, Chapel and church congregations and the communities of Six Bells and the Ebbw Fach Valley.

Guardian represents different things for different people; an awesome piece of art, an amazing feat of engineering and a national landmark.

For those who worked on the project, the families and those affected by the terrible events on the 28th June 1960, it has established not only a fitting tribute but one which will stand proud for generations to come so that all communities affected by the mining industry are not forgotten.

This was a community led project and whilst many agencies supported its creation, it was the drive and determination of the families working with Communities First and its partners who made it happen.

Mair Sheen
Six Bells Communities First Coordinator

GUARDIAN

Guardian is a memorial commissioned by Blaenau Gwent County Borough Council on behalf of the community of Six Bells to commemorate the 50th Anniversary of the Colliery disaster that occurred on the morning of 28th June 1960.

At approximately 10.45, an explosion took place in the West District of the Old Coal Seam, caused by an ignition of firedamp. Coal-dust in the air ignited and the explosion spread almost throughout the district. Killing 45 out of the 48 men who worked in that area of the mine, the tragedy would have been even worse had it not been for maintenance work being carried out on the O.10 face where otherwise 125 men would have been working.

Lethal concentrations of carbon monoxide gas were found to be present.
A public enquiry into the disaster took place, at No 2 Court of Newport Civic Centre, between 19th and 28th September 1960.
The Inspector of Mines reported that the probable cause of the explosion was firedamp ignited by a spark from a stone falling onto a steel girder.

IVOR JAMES BAITON, 48. ROSEHEYWORTH
DANIEL JAMES BANCROFT 'DANNY', 46. SIX BELLS
ROBERT CHARLES BROWN 'ROY', 35. ABERTILLERY
FRANK COOPER, 45. ROSEHEYWORTH
JOSEPH CORBETT 'JOE', 50. ABERTILLERY
THOMAS GEORGE CRANDON 'GEORGE', 46. SIX BELLS
WALTER THOMAS DAVIES 'WALLY', 34. BRYNMAWR
ROYDEN JAMES EDWARDS, 27. SWFFRYD
PERCY GORDON ELSEY, 52. SIX BELLS
ALBERT JOHN EVANS 'AUB', 51. BLAINA
KEITH LEONARD FRAMPTON 'SMILER', 29. SIX BELLS
ALBERT GARDNER, 59. PANTYPWDYN
GEORGE GOLDSPINK 'GOLDY', 37. SIX BELLS
VERNON ALEXANDER GRIFFITHS, FATHER, 42. BRYNITHEL
CLIVE ALAN GRIFFITHS, SON, 18. BRYNITHEL
ERNEST VICTOR HARDING 'VIC', 51. ABERTILLERY
IDRIS JONES, 57. SIX BELLS
JOHN PERCIVAL JONES, 56. ABERTILLERY
JOSEPH JOHN KING 'JACK', 47. ABERTILLERY
DENNIS EDMUND LANE, 19. SIX BELLS
GEORGE HENRY LUFFMAN, 55. BLAINA
TELFORD CECIL MAPP 'CECIL', 42. ABERBEEG
HERBERT AMOS MAYBERRY 'BERT', 55. ABERTILLERY
SIDNEY MOORE 'SID', 54. SIX BELLS
WILLIAM JOHN MORDEN ' BILL', 52. BLAINA
ROY MARTIN MORGAN, FATHER, 44. LLANHILLETH
COLIN REGINALD MORGAN, SON, 22. SIX BELLS
COLIN MALCOLM DONALD MORGAN, 26. ABERTILLERY
ISLWYN MORRIS, 35. ABERTILLERY
WILLIAM HENRY PARTRIDGE 'BILLY', FATHER, 45. BLAINA
ANTHONY VERDUN PARTRIDGE 'TONY', SON, 20. BLAINA
TREVOR PAUL, 25. SIX BELLS
WILFRED ALFRED CHARLES PHIPPS, 60. SIX BELLS
ALFRED GEORGE PINKETT 'GEORGE', 45. ABERTILLERY
FREDRICK REES, 37. ABERTILLERY
WILFRED HUGHES THOMAS ' WILF', 58. NANTYGLO
WILLIAM GLYN REYNOLDS 'BILL', TWIN, 21. BRYNMAWR
MANSEL REYNOLDS, TWIN, 21. SIX BELLS
ARTHUR WATERS, 35. ABERBEEG
PHILLIP JOHN WATKINS 'JACK', 53. ABERBEEG
WILFRED WESTON 'CLUCKY WESTON', 47. ABERTILLERY
FREDRICK WHITE, 58. SIX BELLS
WILLIAM WHITTINGHAM 'BRIGHT EYES', 34. ABERTILLERY
RICHARD JOHN WILLIAMS 'JACK', 51. CWMTILLERY
JOHN WOOSNAM, 24. BOURNEVILLE

28TH JUNE 1960

When I started designing the memorial for Six Bells, I knew nothing of the area or the disaster, which happened the same year I was born. I was initially asked to put forward a proposal that would show the concept and scale of the memorial, and was given a blank canvas.

On my first visit to Six Bells, I was unprepared for the beauty and tranquillity of the former colliery site. It was hard to believe it had ever been a thriving, working pit. Herons flew in to land and fish in the stream, and nothing could be heard except the sound of running water from the nearby culvert.

When I am looking for inspiration to design a sculpture, I take in the whole environment around me and let it inform the decisions I make about size, scale, material and form.

I knew almost as soon as I got back home that whatever idea I put forward, it had to be something that the ordinary person in the community could appreciate and understand - it needed to be a statement that could easily be grasped without having to wade through a mist of confused interpretation - something bold, dynamic and inspiring that could make a connection to the hearts and minds of those for whom it was made.

As an artist I have always been drawn to the classic tradition and particularly the ideals of the Renaissance sculptors who found beauty in the natural form, and is something I have tried to emulate throughout my whole working life. It became quite a straightforward process to come up with the final design - a representation of a working man with arms outstretched - asking so many questions, but mostly 'why?'. A simple yet poignant statement, poetic and eloquent.

I hope the end result speaks for itself, and although the journey to bring the memorial to completion was not without a few challenges, the way in which it has been accepted into the community has made it worth while. What remains for me is the memory of everyone I talked to on the site during the installation who unconditionally understood and accepted 'Guardian' for what it was and what I was trying to do..... thank you.

Sebastien Boyesen

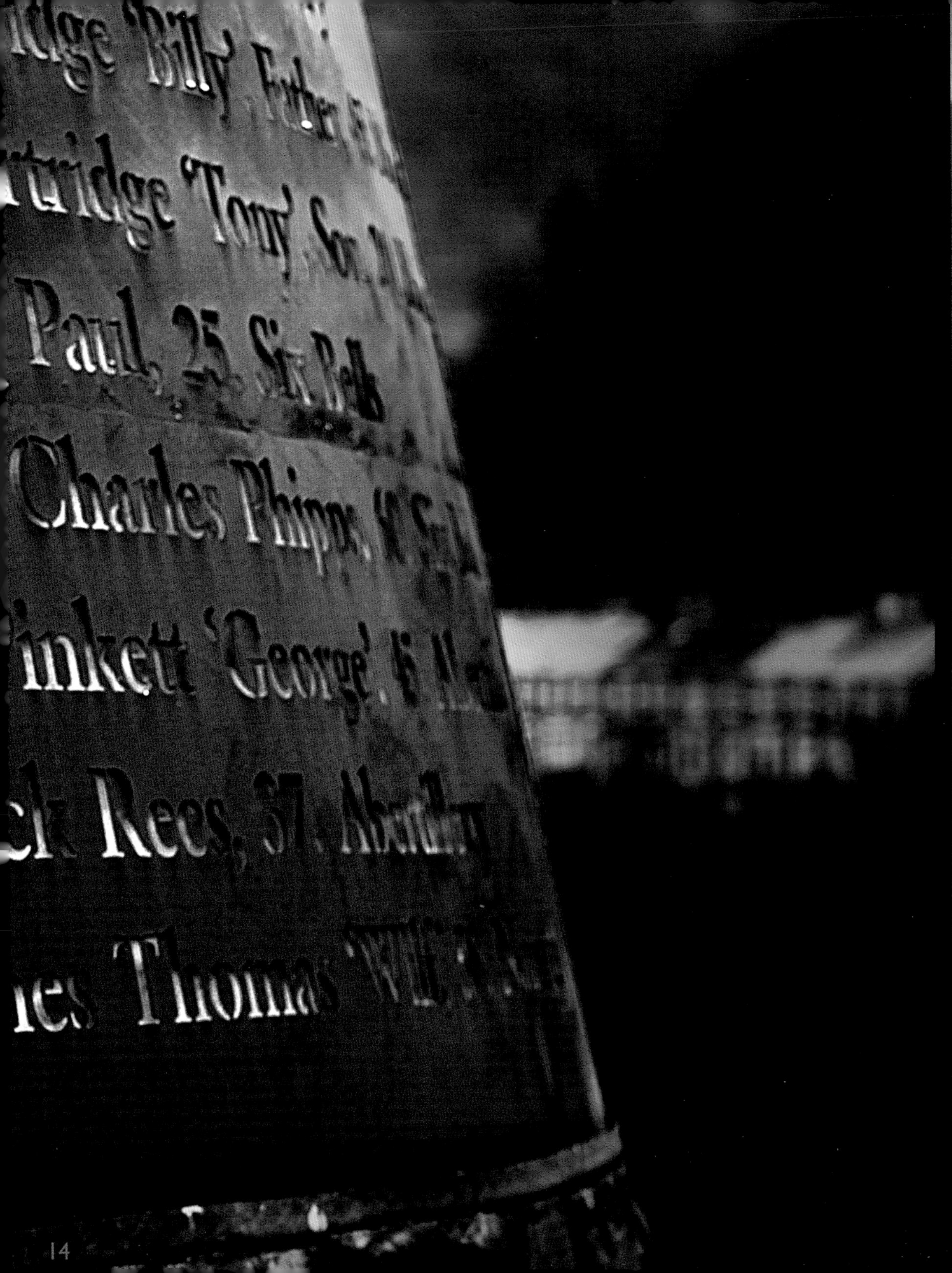
'Tony'
Paul, 25, Six Bells
Charles Phipps
'George'
Rees, 37
Thomas

During the last 30 years I have made many public artworks throughout Wales and the UK, mostly for various Councils as part of urban regeneration schemes.

Experience has shown me that in order for a new work to be valued and accepted by the community for whom it is made, there needs to be an integrated element of research and consultation, so that when the final piece is in place it has meaning and relevance.

For the proposed Six Bells Memorial it was felt that the work had to reflect the wishes and aspirations of the community and family members, so that some form of closure could be realised. It was essential that the memorial achieved this in essence and I felt directly answerable to their feelings, which seemed like a huge responsibilty.

Although consultation is an important part of the development of such a work, the results depend enormously on the level of response and engagement. For Six Bells, part of the research involved setting up a stall in the local shops and town centre and simply talking to as many people as possible, including members of the Mines Rescue who were there on the day, realtives, and anyone who had something to say.

The response was both unprecedented and overwhelming, and I was unprepared for the level of raw emotion that was still felt by all those affected by the disaster. Everyone I spoke to had a story to tell about how their lives had been changed forever. I was struck by how gracious and supportive everyone was and how important they sensed it was to create a fitting memorial for an event, that although it happened 50 years ago, still felt like yesterday.

It was a humbling experience which I can personally say has changed the way in which I perceive the role and value of the public artist, and continues to impact on the work I do on a daily basis.

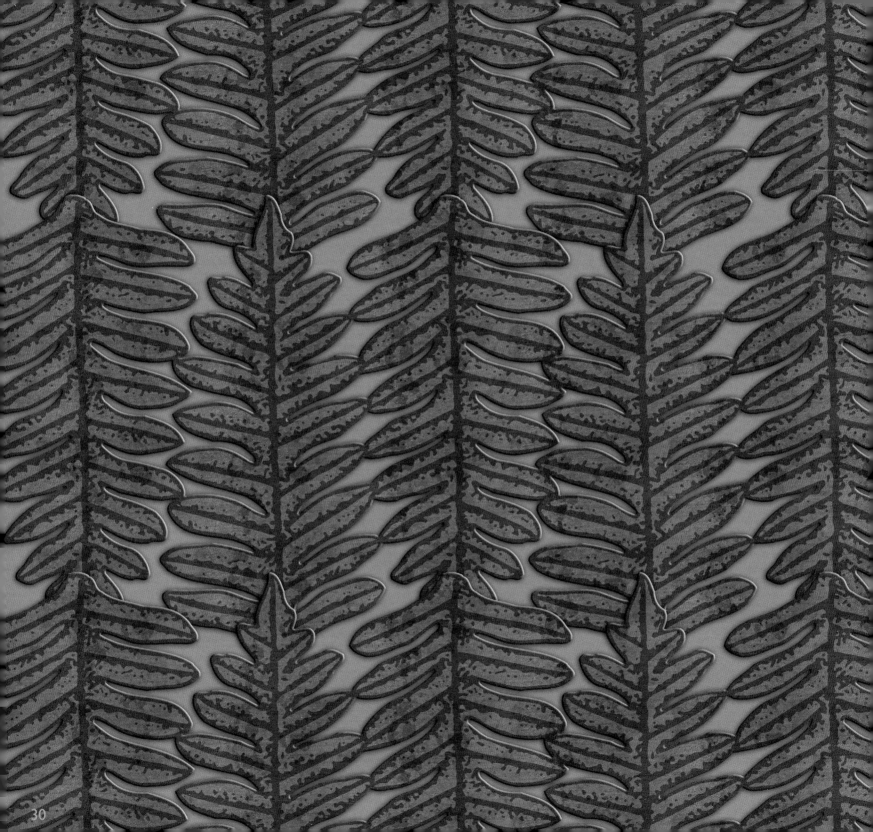

DESIGNING GUARDIAN

The sculpture was a very complex piece to design, requiring a range of technical and computer skills to bring it to life. Although I had made several 'sliced' works before, this took it to a whole new level. The first stage was to research and create the figure as a CAD (Computer Aided Design) model including the helmet and clothes to ensure I had the details correct and typical of those used at the time.

My initial design had shown the figure to be bare-chested, which originally created some controversy. My feelings were that I wanted to show the power and emotion of the figure in its simplest and most pure form - stripped down and uncomplicated.

Using a life-model and 3D scanning technology, I created the figure in a software programme called ZBrush, which is used universally throughout the Film industry for CGI and special effects. This allowed me to 'sculpt' the figure on the computer, which I could then take into other programmes to create the sliced contour sections. It took many months to finalise the CAD data and to lay-out over 20,000 individual sections to be laser cut out at a factory. Every single piece had a unique reference number, along with a colour code to help identify which section and layer it belonged to.

Originally, Guardian was intended to be made from small component pieces such as leaves or mechanical shapes welded together - almost like a mesh. An early proposal looked at making the entire sculpture from the names of those who had died, but this was felt to be too difficult to read.

Finally after creating models of different full-size sections, a visit was made to the studio by the Six Bells Steering Group to view how the models might work in reality. It became apparent that the 'sliced' and 'layered' approach seemed to be more effective at capturing the detail, and the decision was made to go with this option. It was also felt that the layered technique echoed the geological strata of the coalfields themselves.

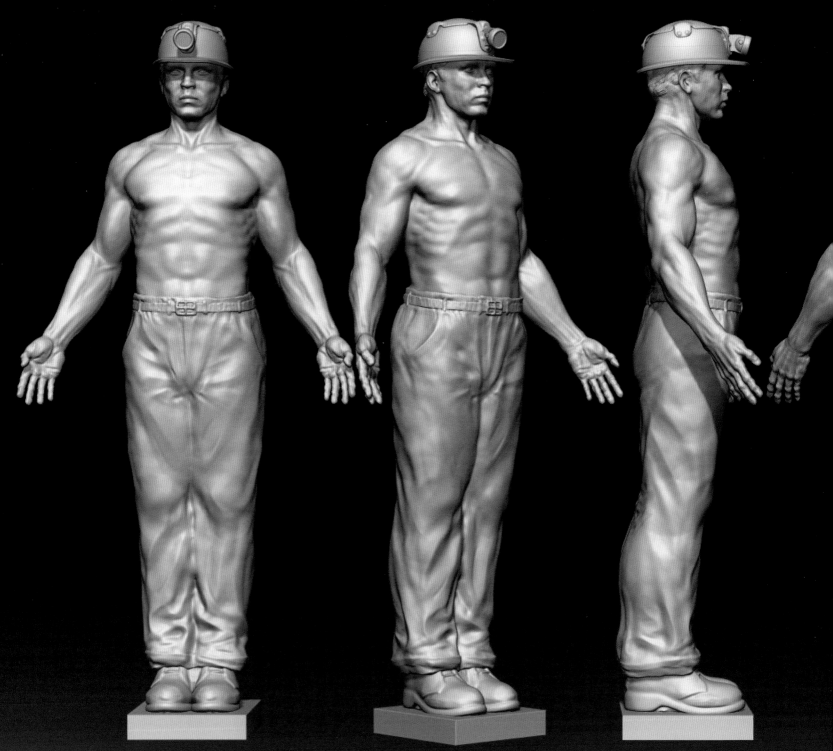

The final render of the 3D ZBrush model, ready to be 'sliced' into layers and contours.

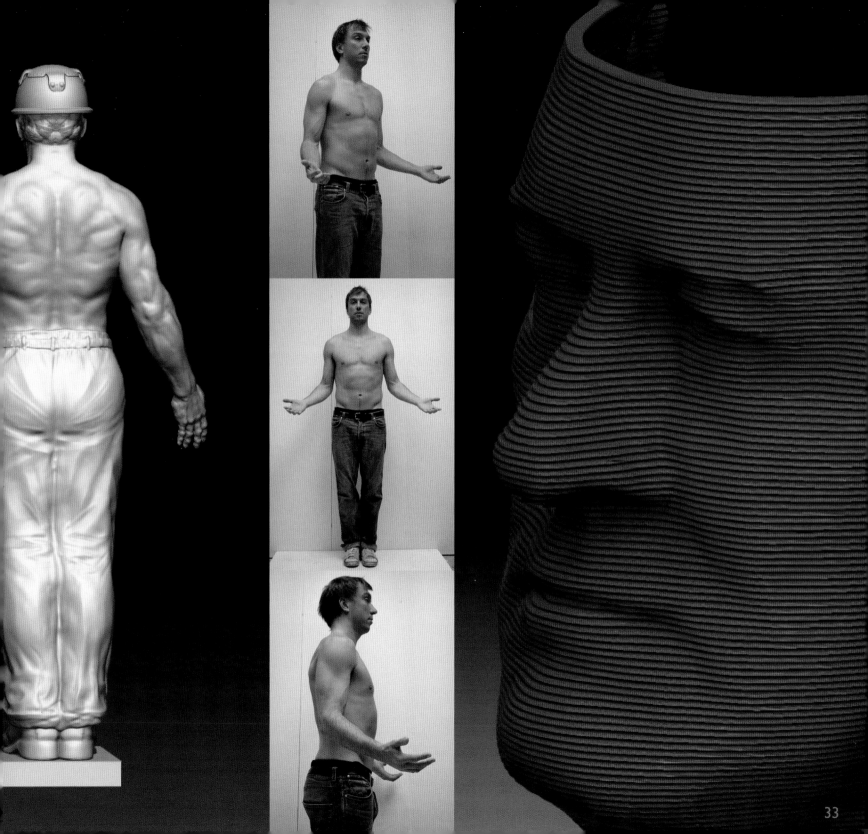

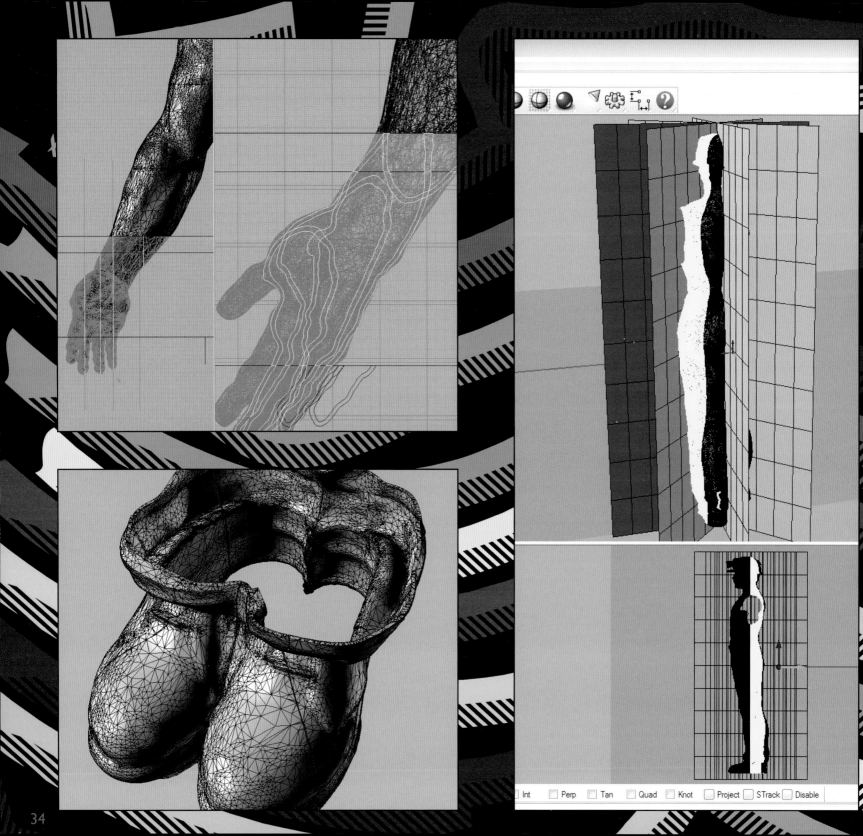

Int ☐ Perp ☐ Tan ☐ Quad ☐ Knot ☐ Project ☐ STrack ☐ Disable

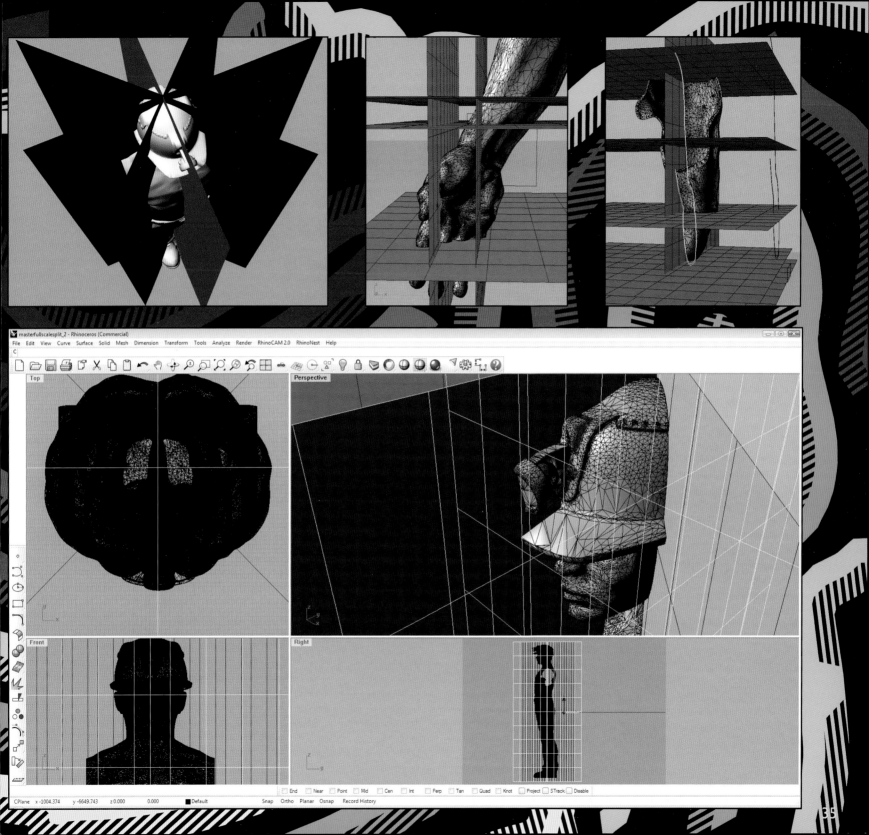

Different surface treatments and patterns were initially considered.

Early visualisation of the Guardian at a different location to the final site,
which was roughly a 100 metres further along the former colliery site, past the pond area.

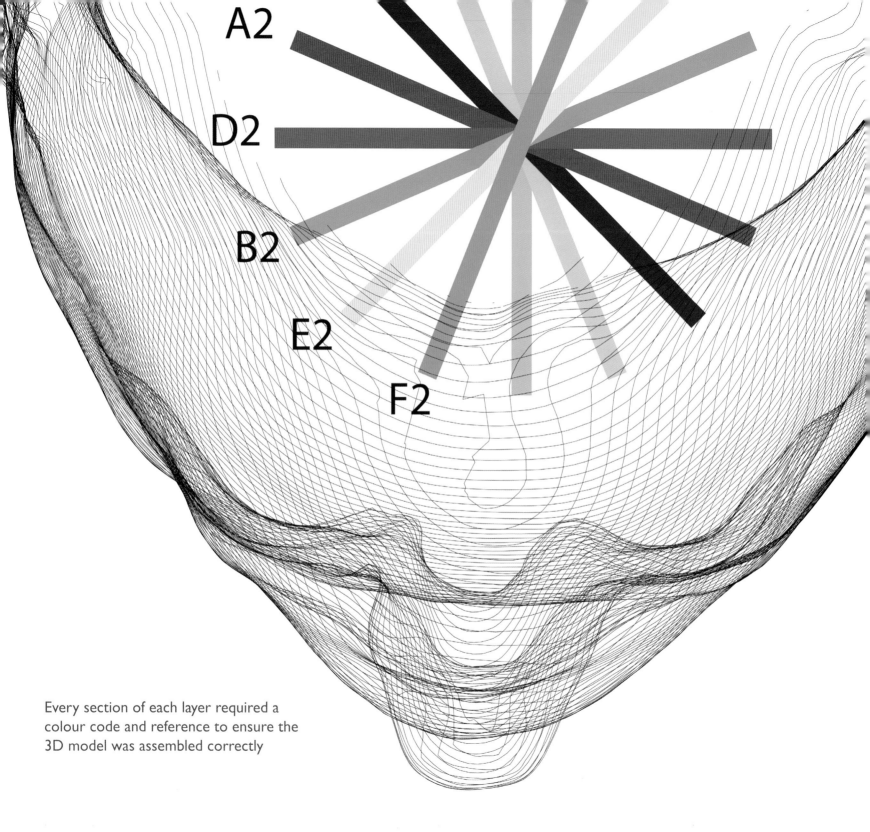

A2

D2

B2

E2

F2

Every section of each layer required a
colour code and reference to ensure the
3D model was assembled correctly

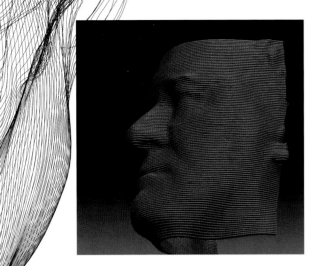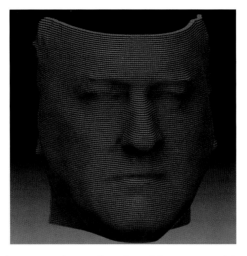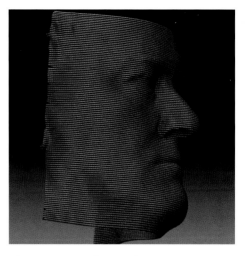

CAD test renders and models to see how the sliced layers would work to create the sculpture.

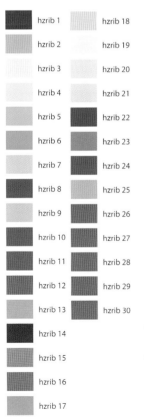

hzrib 1	hzrib 18
hzrib 2	hzrib 19
hzrib 3	hzrib 20
hzrib 4	hzrib 21
hzrib 5	hzrib 22
hzrib 6	hzrib 23
hzrib 7	hzrib 24
hzrib 8	hzrib 25
hzrib 9	hzrib 26
hzrib 10	hzrib 27
hzrib 11	hzrib 28
hzrib 12	hzrib 29
hzrib 13	hzrib 30
hzrib 14	
hzrib 15	
hzrib 16	
hzrib 17	

MAKING GUARDIAN

Guardian was fabricated at the Boyesen Studio in Llangrannog, West Wales.
The thousands of contour strips, each with a unique reference code, were assembled on
to vertical 'Ribs' that ran from top to bottom, providing the spacing between each layer.
The material used is a special steel that is designed to rust on the surface and create a
protective layer. Known as Cor-Ten, it was originally developed by the United States Steel
Corporation for the Railways in the 1930's, and has since been used for many architectural
applications and sculptures.

A small team of people were required to assemble and organise the fabrication process,
which took over six months, working seven days a week.
In charge of the welding was Saskia Harrison. Workshop manager was Simon Wilkins
who had responsibility for coordinating the overall build and fabrication.
Matt Cox and Simon Turnock sorted out and referenced all the component pieces.

As each section was assembled and welded together, it was then stacked onto the next section
to ensure that it fitted properly. Joining and locating lugs were welded into place at this stage.
Although the workshop is in a beautiful seaside location, it meant that the size of each piece
had to remain small enough to be transported down a narrow track and over a bridge to a
waiting lorry half a mile away.

The fabrication of Guardian required over 200 sheets of Cor-Ten steel to make the 20,000
slices and 5 miles of welding wire. The overall height of the sculpture is 20 metres, or 66 feet,
including a 7.4 metre plinth and weighs approximately 8 tonnes.

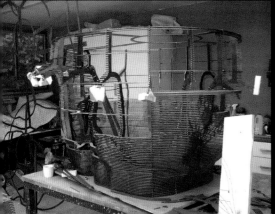

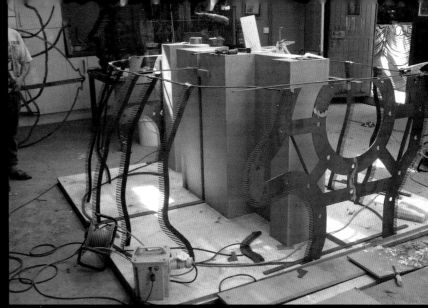

INSTALLING GUARDIAN

Installation of the sculpture began on the morning of the 24th June 2010, with the plinth having already been constructed in the previous months. Guardian was delivered on a flat bed lorry in sections, limited by the size we could get out of the workshop in Llangrannog. The next few days consisted of extremely long hours, as each section was carefully craned into position. The arms had still not arrived, and were being frantically completed by Simon and Saskia.

The sections went together relatively easily, although there were times when things appeared to frustrate every effort to get them to line up properly. The pressure of having only a few days left before the unveiling meant that failure just wasn't an option, and every technical challenge had to be overcome. All of the fitting work was done from the inside of the growing sculpture, where a crude series of platforms had been installed, meaning that as each section was lifted into place, a new platform could be built from which to work. No external scaffolding was used during construction.

The arms, weighing over a tonne each, were scheduled to be attached on the day before the unveiling, and were finally delivered to site. However, It soon became apparent that a series of insurmountable problems stood in the way of successfully installing them. Due to the complex technical nature of the structure and the difficulty involved in craning them into position, it was realised that it was too dangerous to attempt the work under such conditions, and reluctantly it was agreed (probably the hardest decision I have ever made) that we would have to leave the arms off until after the unveiling. Final completion was a month later.

UNVEILING GUARDIAN

Guardian was dedicated as part of a Commemoration Service on the 28th June 2010 led by the Archbishop of Canterbury, Reverend Rowan Williams.

Relatives of the victims, the survivors of the disaster and those involved in the rescue teams were among those remembering them as the memorial featuring the names, age and home town of all who died was unveiled.

More than 7,500 people attended the memorial service on the former colliery site to pay tribute to the 45 miners killed in an explosion there 50 years ago.

Paying tribute to the men, the Archbishop of Canterbury, Dr Rowan Williams led a moving memorial service, including a one minute silence and a reading of the names of the victims.

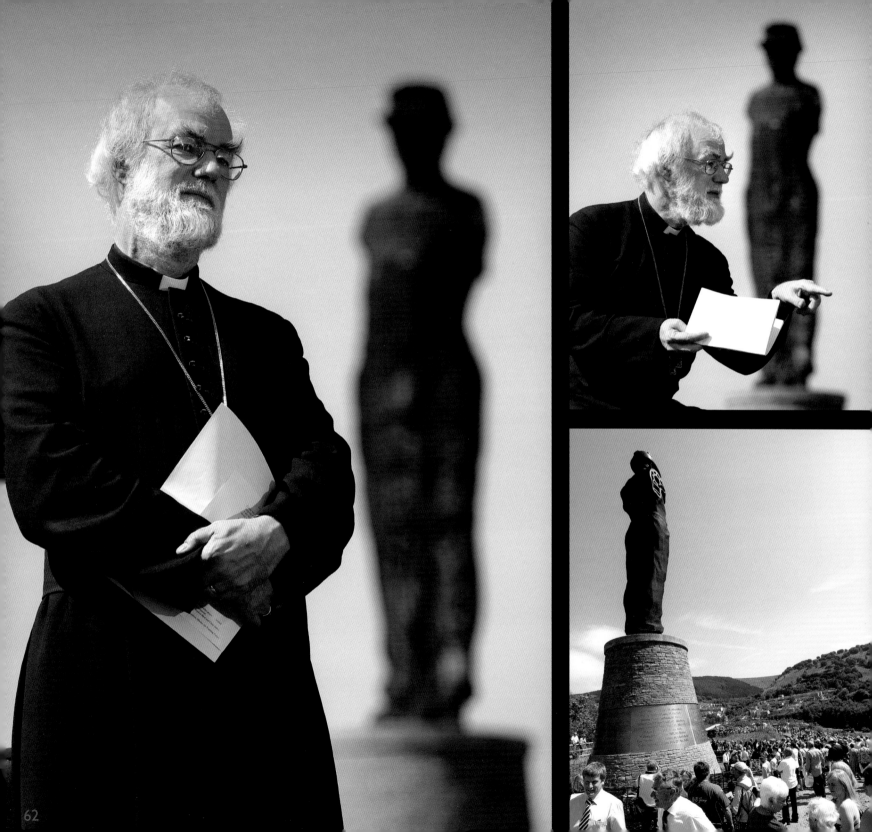

HRH Prince Charles visiting Guardian and Tŷ Ebbw Fach on the 21st November 2011

SPECIAL THANKS TO:
Guardian was a truly epic undertaking and were it
not for the help, support and understanding of the
following, it might never have happened.

Mair Sheen, Aimée Goulding and Bethan Trapnell - Six Bells Communities First Team
Six Bells Steering Group
Six Bells Communities First Partnership Board
Six Bells Regeneration Team
Blaenau Gwent County Borough Council
Abertillery and Llanhilleth Community Council
Simon Wilkins - main fabrication and workshop manager
Saskia Harrison - Firefox welding
Jake Bath - installation and site work
Matt Cox - workshop technician
Simon Turnock - workshop technician
Mike Murphy & Daughters - transport and logistics
Robert Price Builders Merchants, Abertillery
Paul's Scaffolding Ltd
Barry Evans Metalwork - Plinth formwork
Hanson Concrete
Dai Trapnell at Big Pit - Head scan
The Big Pit - Research
Phil Blackwood - Model
T & C Stonemasonry
Paul Read & Terry Thomas, Altron - Laser cutting
M & E Pearce Ltd - Fixings
Brynhoffnant Plant Hire - Loading
Melanie Lindsell - BBC Wales
Steff Jenkins - Urdd Llangrannog
Stephen Micallef / GA Spacey Structural Engineers
Steven Guevara - CAD support
Rhino - CAD Software
Zbrush - CAD Software
Tube and Steel Supplies - Newport
Glen Metals - Cor-Ten
Leta Engineering and Plant Co. Ltd.

The Families and Communities of Six Bells and Blaenau Gwent

PHOTO CREDITS

It has taken over three years since the unveiling of Guardian to
find the time and space to put a book together of all the photos
that were taken of the project.
Fortunately, the ensuing years meant that the seasons changed and
photos were taken at different times of the day and year, by different
people, with the most beautiful results.
I tracked down a number of these talented photographers who had published
on-line and asked permission for their photos to be included in this book,
and without exception everyone agreed, for which I am grateful.

I would, however, like to single out Dai Smith for additional thanks, for his brooding
and atmospheric pictures, without which I would not have a book to publish.

Also Patrick Olner for recording the challenging process of installing the sculpture!

Dai Smith - front cover, 2, 5-19, 26, 27
Patrick Olner - 22 mid, 23, 46-65
Thomas Wayne - 4, 20
HDC Photography - 24
John Selway 28, 29
Paula James - 25
Steve Davies - 21
Tracey Matthews - 22
Sarah Hopkins - inner sleeve
All other photographs by the artist

For more information about Guardian, please visit; www.guardianwales.info

Dai Smith Photos; daismiff39@hotmail.com   Flickr; www.flickr.com/photos/10141102@N08/
Patrick Olner Photos; www.tallandshort.co.uk
HDC Photography; www.hdcymru.com
John Selway; www.jselwayphotography.com
Thomas Wayne; www.flickr.com/photos/thomaswayne/
Sarah Hopkins Photography; www.sarahhopkinsphotography.co.uk
Stephen Davies; www.flickr.com/23125051@N04
Tracey Matthews; www.flickr.com/photos/71060747@N06
Paula James; www.flickr.com/photos/paulajjames